Julius Caesar

by Jan Goldberg

Julius Caesar
by Jan Goldberg

Illustrations by Dan Bridy

Photography: p. 7 © Christie's Images/CORBIS; p. 10 © Christie's Images/CORBIS; p. 15 © Werner Forman/CORBIS; p. 22 © Bettmann/CORBIS; p. 23 © Bettmann/CORBIS; p. 30 © Bettmann/CORBIS; p. 35 © Sandro Vannini/CORBIS; p. 37 © Christie's Images/CORBIS; p. 48 © Bettmann/CORBIS; p. 54 © Bettmann/CORBIS; p. 56 © Albert Charles August Racinet/Wood River Gallery/Picture Quest; p. 61 © Michael Nicholson/CORBIS; p. 64 © Bettmann/CORBIS; p. 65 © Bettmann/CORBIS; p. 67 © Bettmann/CORBIS; p. 71 © Bettmann/CORBIS; p. 74 © Sandro Vannini/CORBIS; p. 78 © Bettmann/CORBIS; p. 84 © Bettmann/CORBIS; p. 88 © Bettmann/CORBIS; p. 89 © Bettmann/CORBIS; p. 93 © Bettmann/CORBIS

Nonfiction Reviewer
John Barell, Ed.D.
Educational Consultant, The American Museum of Natural History
New York City

Art Buying by Inkwell Publishing Solutions, Inc., New York City

Cover Design by Inkwell Publishing Solutions, Inc., New York City

ISBN: 0-7367-1800-1

Copyright © Zaner-Bloser, Inc.

All rights reserved. No part of this book may be reproduced or transmitted in any form or by any means, electronic or mechanical, including photocopying, recording, or by any information storage and retrieval system, without permission in writing from the Publisher.

Web sites have been carefully researched for accuracy, content, and appropriateness. However, Web sites are subject to change. Internet usage should always be monitored.

Zaner-Bloser, Inc., P.O. Box 16764, Columbus, Ohio 43216-6764, 1-800-421-3018

Printed in China

03 04 05 06 07 (321) 5 4 3 2 1

TABLE OF CONTENTS

Introduction 1
Chapter One: Life in Ancient Rome 3
Chapter Two: Young Julius Caesar 17
Chapter Three: Caesar Enters the
    Political Arena 24
Chapter Four: Climbing the Political Ladder 34
Chapter Five: The Triumvirate 46
Chapter Six: The Gallic Wars 54
Chapter Seven: The Civil War 67
Chapter Eight: Caesar's Final Battle:
    The Fall of the Roman Republic 81
Chapter Nine: The Legacy of Julius Caesar 91

Time Line of Major Events 97
Bibliography 99
Glossary 102
Index 104

The Roman Empire at the time of Caesar's birth

INTRODUCTION

Imagine yourself in a time machine. The date is set for March 15, 44 B.C. The place is the Roman Senate. When you arrive, you expect to find a busy room full of senators making laws for the good of Rome. Instead, the room is empty. You hear the distant sound of sobbing coming from another room. A shredded purple toga lies in the corner.

Had you arrived a few minutes earlier, the scene would have been one of confusion and fear. An assassination has just taken place, and now one of the most powerful men in the world is dead. Julius Caesar, dictator and ruler of the Roman Empire, has died at the hands of a few jealous Romans.

During his lifetime, Julius Caesar lived in a great city, traveled extensively, and gained enormous wealth and power. In a world where most people never left their villages and lived with very little money, Julius Caesar lived a privileged life.

Caesar accomplished many feats that many thought were impossible. He was a brilliant general, a skillful politician, a talented writer, and a great speaker. His conquests in battle greatly expanded the Roman Empire, and he knew how to win the favor of the Roman people.

But there was another side to Caesar, and it probably cost him his life. Above all other things, Caesar loved power. In order to gain that power, he was willing to start wars, steal, bribe officials, and destroy ancient forms of government.

Julius Caesar dared to be the sole ruler of Rome. He brought an end to the Roman Republic and founded a government based on one man's rule—his own. You already know how the story ends, but to get there, it takes many exciting twists and turns. Along the way, there are battles, pirates, queens, and sinister plots. In order to understand the rest of the story, you are going to have to get out of your time machine and learn a little bit more about the people and culture of ancient Rome.

CHAPTER ONE
LIFE IN ANCIENT ROME

According to legend, the twin sons of the war god, Mars, founded Rome. Their names were Romulus and Remus. When the twins were born, they were abandoned on the banks of the Tiber River. A wolf came upon the boys and cared for them until they were rescued by shepherds. The boys grew up in the hills overlooking the river. One day, Romulus and Remus got into a terrible quarrel over who would rule the land. Remus was killed, and Romulus named the city after himself.

Romulus and Remus were rescued by shepherds.

As you can see, the legend gave Rome a great and fierce beginning. Unfortunately, the real story isn't quite as exciting. The city grew out of small villages along the banks of the Tiber River in Italy. The people who lived in the area were called *Latins,* but once the villages merged into one city, they became known as *Romans.*

For a long time kings ruled Rome, but eventually people grew tired of having one ruler, and they formed a type of government called a **republic**. In the Roman Republic, two officials, known as *consuls,* were advised by the Senate, a group of appointed and elected lawmakers.

The Roman Class System

Roman society was very organized. People were divided into citizens and slaves. Citizens had rights and duties that were not given to slaves. They could vote in elections and serve in the army. They were also expected to pay taxes.

The citizens of Rome were then divided into three classes. The class that they were born into was usually the one they remained in for life. This worked well for the wealthy class, but the poorer people in the city were very discontented. No matter how hard the average citizen worked, he or she could not become a landowner or have much say in how the government was run.

Patricians (puh•**trish**•uhnz) were the wealthiest and most aristocratic people of Rome. They held the important political, religious, and legal positions. In order to be in the Senate, a Roman had to be a patrician. Because of this, the patricians were the ones who made the laws in Rome. Most historians agree that their greediness weakened and corrupted the government of the republic.

The equites (**ek**•wi•teez) were the powerful middle class of Rome. They included businessmen, traders, and bankers. Because they had money, they were often landowners. Many of the equites who were traders brought goods into Rome from other countries like Egypt and China.

Ordinary citizens were called *plebeians* (pli•**bee**•uhnz). About ninety percent of the citizens of Rome were in this class. They were the farmers, fishermen, crafters, and soldiers. It was often difficult for these citizens to find work. Rome had so many slaves to do the work for free that the plebeians were often without work.

Rome relied heavily on slave labor. Slaves were not considered citizens of Rome.

What About Roman Women?

Roman women were considered citizens of Rome. However, like in many other ancient societies, they did not enjoy the same rights as male citizens. As you may have guessed, Roman women were not able to vote. In the early years of Rome, women had very few rights. However, during Caesar's time things were beginning to improve for women.

Eventually, women gained the right to inherit and control their own property and to file for divorce. In most households, instead of servants, they became partners with their husbands. Roman women regularly attended parties and public functions with their husbands. In the ancient world, it was very unusual for women to enjoy the type of freedom that the women of Rome had.

Thousands of prisoners from Greece and other conquered lands worked as slaves in homes, fields, mines, workshops, and building projects. Not all slaves were treated badly. Educated Greek slaves were highly valued as tutors, and some became very influential. Some slaves earned wages and saved money to buy their freedom. They were known as *freedmen*.

So, though Rome was a flourishing metropolis for some, in numerous parts of the city, discontent was widespread. Unrest and **civil war** were common. Many poor and desperate people wondered how they would survive.

Roman Homes

The type of housing a family lived in was also determined by their social class. In large cities such as Rome, the price

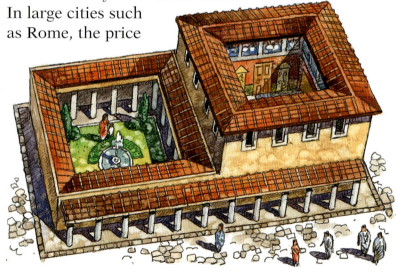

The homes of the wealthy had many of the same conveniences we have today.

of a house was too high for the average citizen to afford. Most people lived in rooms or apartments called *insulae* (**in**•suh•lee). Apartments were located in private homes, above shops or factories, or in houses that were turned into multifamily dwellings.

The Complaints of an Apartment Dweller

Many Roman authors wrote about the poor conditions that the plebeians had to endure. Here is what one writer had to say:

"We live in a city which is, to a great extent, propped up by flimsy boards. The manager of your apartment building stands in front of the collapsing structure and, while he conceals a gaping crack, he tells you to sleep well—even though a total cave-in is imminent! It's best, of course, to live where there are not fires and no panics in the dead of night. Here, one neighbor discovers a fire and shouts for water, another neighbor moves out his shabby possessions. The third floor where you live, is already smoking—but you don't even know! Downstairs there is panic, but you, upstairs, where the gentle pigeons nest, where only thin tiles protect you from the rain, you will be the last to know."

—Juvenal

The poorest families generally lived on the top floor in the smallest apartments. They were built of wood and were very drafty. Most apartments did not have running water. Instead, people went to the nearby public fountains and carried heavy jars of water home.

The common people of Rome did not eat as well as the upper class. Most apartments did not have kitchens. It was against the law to cook in them because the apartments caught fire easily. The average Roman either had to eat cold meals or buy hot food from the many take-out food shops. These meals often consisted of wheat and barley porridge, bread, vegetables, olives, grapes, and cheap cuts of meat that were made into sausages or pies.

Houses for the wealthy had many of the same conveniences we have today. They had bedrooms, bathrooms with running water, a library, a kitchen, and a dining room. The houses were furnished lavishly with carpets, wall hangings, and marble.

In their kitchens, they prepared three meals a day. Breakfast was usually bread and fruit. At midday, they ate a light lunch of bread, cheese, cold fish, meat, and vegetables. The main meal of the day

Did You Know?

What would you say if your mother told you that she was fixing rodents for dinner? Dormice are small squirrel-like rodents that were very common in ancient Rome. They were also a very popular Roman dish. They were served with honey and poppy seeds.

was a three-course dinner served in the evening. This meal usually consisted of a starter of eggs, seafood, or snails; a main course of roast or boiled meat; and a last course of sweets and fruit.

The Roman Family

Family was important to all Romans, no matter which class they belonged to. The word *family* comes from the Latin word *familia,* which means "household." In Roman times, that is exactly what a family was. Most families had a father, a mother, children, and grandparents. Some also included slaves, freedmen, cousins, uncles, aunts, and adopted children.

In a Roman family, the father was the head of the household. He held the power of life and death over everyone in the household, including his wife. In most cases, however, this power was never actually used. When a baby was just a few days old, it was shown to the father. If the father took the baby into his arms, the child was named and became a part of the family.

The daily running of the household was left to the women. They were encouraged not to have jobs outside the home. Instead, they were expected to raise the children and take care of the house. They spent a lot of time spinning thread from wool to make clothes.

Children were expected to grow up quickly. Poor children sometimes had to start work as young as five or six years old in order to help support the family.

These children often worked along with their parents. Children of wealthier parents spent their time playing until they started school at the age of seven.

Roman parents had to provide an education for their children. There was no free education in Rome. Fathers taught their sons how to swim, run, and handle weapons. Mothers showed their daughters how to spin wool and keep house.

Wealthy Romans could afford to provide a better education for their children. Often, they entrusted their

Wealthy Roman children were educated by pedagogues.

children's education to special slaves called *pedagogues* (**ped•uh•gogs**). Some children stayed home for their education, and some went to school with other students.

In Rome, there were three levels of education for the wealthier children. From the age of 7 to 12, students learned reading, writing, and math. Most girls left school at this point and got married. When boys turned 12, they spent 5 years reading great works of literature and learning to write. At the age of 17, students went to study with a **rhetorician** (ret•uh•rish•uhn), a master of writing and public speaking. After completing their studies, these young men often went on to serve in the Roman government.

Slavery

Slaves were another vital part of wealthy Roman families. Many of these slaves became significant, outspoken, trusted, and even loved members of Roman households. Slaves cooked meals, took care of children, prepared for entertaining, and did all of the day-to-day household chores. For the most part, they were treated well. The patricians and equites had at least five to ten slaves. But the very wealthy owned sixty, seventy, or even hundreds of slaves.

While slavery is a horrible and inhumane practice no matter where it exists, it was an accepted way of life in the ancient world. Romans treated their slaves fairly well compared to other civilizations. Household slaves often lived in better conditions than the plebeians.

The Gods of the Empire

Pagan (**pay**•guhn) religion played a very important part in everyday Roman life. In fact, every house had its own shrine to the household gods. The family offered gifts of wine, bread, and fruit to ensure that the household would be protected from such misfortunes as robbery, fire, hunger, and bad luck. The Romans prayed to these pagan gods when they woke up and when they left the house.

There were many gods and spirits in Rome—about 30,000 in all. These gods were thought to watch over different aspects of the Romans' lives, and the people were afraid of them. They believed that if the gods were pleased, they would have good luck. But they thought that the gods could be easily angered. Priests looked for signs that the gods were unhappy. Thunder and lightning were bad **omens**. After death, people believed they went to a place called *Hades* (**hay**•deez).

Did You Know?

The Romans thought that when a person died, his or her spirit was ferried to Hades across an underground river called the *Styx*. At funerals, a coin was placed under the dead person's tongue to pay the ferry fare.

The most important Roman gods were Jupiter, ruler of gods and men and king of heaven; his wife Juno, queen of heaven and goddess of women and marriage; and Jupiter's daughter Minerva, goddess of wisdom and art. The gods of the Romans were similar to the Greek gods, but they had different names.

The Romans built temples as homes to their gods. Inside each temple, there was a shrine with a statue that represented the god's human form. Only priests who served the god were allowed inside the temple. Worshipers had to worship outside. They did not attend the temples regularly, but only when they wanted to ask the god for something.

People worshiped the gods through prayer and offerings of food and wine. It was very important that prayers to the gods were said correctly. The Romans believed that their prayers would be granted only if they were said in exactly the right way. So, while the priest read the prayer out loud, another man checked to see that he was doing it correctly, and a third man played a flute to drown out other noises.

Predicting the future was another important part of Roman religion. The Romans believed that the gods sent messages to warn of coming disasters or as a sign of good luck. Priests called *augurs* examined the insides of dead animals and observed birds, which they believed were messengers from the gods.

> ### DID YOU KNOW?
> The priests used chickens to predict the future. When the chickens were eating well, it was thought that the gods were sending a message of good fortune. When they ate poorly, it was thought to be a sign of impending doom. These chickens were often brought along on battles. When the chickens didn't eat, the army would retreat.

Entertainment

Roman life was full of different types of entertainment. Many of the things the Romans did for entertainment are similar to the things we do today. They went to the theater, watched sporting events, played games, and listened to music.

After a hard day's work, Romans enjoyed relaxing in the bathhouse. Because very few houses in Rome had bathrooms, people went to the public baths. The bathhouses cost very little, so all but the poorest of citizens could afford them. Here they could bathe, get a massage, and chat with their friends. The Roman Baths became important places for people to catch up on daily events and socialize.

Did You Know?

Romans didn't have soap! Instead, they used olive oil. To get themselves clean, they rubbed oil on their bodies and scraped it off with a curved metal tool called a *strigil*.

Knucklebone was a popular game at the baths. Players used the small six-sided anklebones of sheep. They threw the bones up into the air and tried to catch them on the back of the hand. Romans also enjoyed playing marbles and board games. Unfortunately, no rule books survived, so we don't really know how the games were played.

Many of the toys and games that Romans liked to play were represented in paintings and artwork from that time period. We know that Romans had scooters, jump ropes, kites, yo-yos, and swings. Other popular toys appear to have been wooden or clay animals on wheels that children pulled behind them. Some children rode in small carts hitched to the family goat, dog, or pony.

The theater was also a popular form of entertainment. Many of the plays were Greek dramas and comedies. But there were also Roman playwrights. The actors wore facemasks to help project their voices in the huge theaters because they did not have microphones. The type of mask gave the audience clues about the story. Actors wore red wigs to play slaves, and they wore purple clothes to play young men. Women often acted in the plays because men were busy with sporting events.

A statue immortalizing the ancient game of knucklebone

There was nothing the Romans enjoyed more than a good sporting event. During Julius Caesar's time, many of these events were held in an arena called the *Circus Maximus*. The Circus Maximus was large enough to entertain massive numbers of Romans. It could seat approximately 250,000 spectators. Many popular events took place there, including fights, track racing, trick riding, and chariot races.

It was said by one Roman writer that the Roman people only really cared about two things: bread and the circus. The upper class of Rome knew that when the common people were entertained, they would be happy. Politicians often sponsored games in order to win the favor of the plebeians.

CHAPTER TWO

YOUNG JULIUS CAESAR

Chapter One tells of the Rome that Julius Caesar was born into. It was a city of more than half a million people, and its empire stretched from Spain to Asia Minor and from southern France to northern Africa. Rome was the largest city in the western world, and its rise to power was fueled by much ambition. No one realized the birth of Julius Caesar would one day take that ambition to a level that would change Rome forever.

Young Caesar

It all began on a hot summer day in the year 100 B.C. A young woman named Aurelia gave birth to a son. Aurelia's husband, Gaius, was a patrician who served in the Roman Senate. The baby was born into a comfortable household in a section of Rome called *Subura*.

On the ninth day after the baby's birth, a celebration was held. The household gods were honored, and the baby was given a name. The first name would be the same as his father's, Gaius, followed by Julius and the family name of Caesar. Friends and relatives probably stopped by to bring gifts and congratulate the family.

A Roman naming ceremony

What's in a Name?

You could tell a lot about a Roman just by his name. A free Roman male had three parts to his name. The first part indicated his social rank and status. Names, such as Julius, ending in *-ius* (or variations like *-eius* or *-aius*) were reserved for *patricians*, or the wealthiest, most powerful class. Less prestigious endings were *-acus*, *-enus*, and *-ca*.

Roman men also had two other names. One of them was the family name, and one was the name used to identify the individual person. For example, Gaius Julius Caesar—Gaius was his given name, Julius referred to his social class, and Caesar was the name of his family.

Caesar's father was a descendent of the Julii family. They claimed they could trace their roots all the way back to Venus, the Roman goddess of love. Aurelia's family claimed to be among the descendents of an important priest to the sun god. But being a member of the Senate and having well-known ancestors did not hold the power that it once had for Gaius. Before Caesar was born, the family's position improved because of his aunt's marriage to Gaius Marius, an important political leader. While they had lost much of their power over the years, the young Julius Caesar was certainly a member of a prominent Roman family.

B.C. and A.D.

B.C. is used to pinpoint a date that is a particular number of years before the birth of Jesus Christ. The designation is used after the date. For example, Julius Caesar was born in 100 B.C. (Hint: As the years pass, the numbers will get smaller.)

A.D. is used to designate a date that is a particular number of years after the birth of Jesus Christ. The abbreviation refers to anno Domini, or "year of our Lord." It is used before the date rather than after. For example, Augustus died in A.D. 14. (Hint: As the years pass, the numbers will get larger.)

The Education of a Future Leader

Caesar's childhood was typical of most other Roman children. He probably spent his days playing games and driving around in his goat cart imagining himself as the great general he would one day become. The young Caesar was taken care of by his mother and the household slaves.

His father taught the young boy to respect authority and began grooming him to carry on the family name.

By about the age of seven, Caesar began his schooling at home. Aurelia taught him reading and writing in Latin and Greek. Gaius focused on physical activities like wrestling, swimming, and javelin throwing. Both of his parents took their son's education very seriously. They were determined their only son would bring them back to their rightful place in society.

As the young Caesar grew, his education was passed on to a tutor. Caesar's parents wanted to make sure they chose the right person for their son. Usually, well-educated Greek slaves tutored noble boys. But Caesar's parents wanted him to be tutored by a freedman. Thus, a gentle scholar, Marcus Antonius Gnipho (**nee•foh**), from northern Italy, was chosen for the job.

It was with Gnipho that Caesar learned to love knowledge. Each day the tutor told him exciting stories about the literature and history of Rome and other ancient civilizations. Caesar loved to sit and listen to the tutor's stories, and in the process, he became an excellent student. Gnipho also taught Caesar arithmetic, philosophy, Greek, Latin, and law.

Each day after school, Caesar looked forward to horseback riding with his friends. He was said to be an excellent rider who loved to show off by riding as fast as he could with his hands behind his head. He made friends easily and socialized with many other Roman nobles. It was probably here, among his childhood friends, that Caesar prepared himself to be a Roman soldier.

Another pastime of Caesar's was to sit in front of the closed doors of the Senate and eavesdrop on his father's debates with other lawmakers. Gaius stressed to his son that Rome and the well-being of its citizens should always come first. He also taught his son that public opinion and political connections were important to survival in the Senate. Caesar listened carefully to his father's advice. He loved standing at the doors of what he considered to be the most powerful room in the world—and he wanted to enter it.

Young Caesar often eavesdropped outside the doors of the Senate.

Caesar Begins His Career

If Caesar was going to have a career in politics, it was important for him to become a good *orator* (**or**•uh•tuhr), or speaker. Speechmaking was considered a very important skill. In order to win people over to their side, ambitious Romans needed to be able to offer very convincing arguments to encourage others to support their views. As he got older, Caesar worked hard to develop his oratory skills.

Unfortunately, entrance into the political arena of Rome was based on age. Talent did not mean as much as family, experience, and training. During Caesar's youth, a young man had to be thirty years old to hold any important job in the Roman government. To the 15-year-old Caesar, the wait must have seemed like forever.

When Caesar was 15, Gaius died. The young boy was now the head of his family. Members of the family decided that Caesar should pursue a religious career as a priest. It was a very important position. Because Caesar knew that he would be prohibited from entering public life, he did not keep the position long. Instead, he chose to take up a political career.

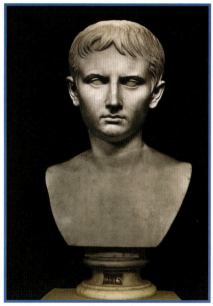

A **bust** of young Julius Caesar

Caesar knew that he must wait to join the Senate, but in the meantime, he decided to build the foundation for his career in politics. He made his first move by entering into a very political marriage with Cornelia, the daughter of a powerful Roman leader named Lucius Cornelius Cinna. Very little is known about Cornelia, but we do know that it was a marriage intended to further Caesar's career. When he got married, Caesar was only 16 years old.

A Roman wedding ceremony

A Marriage Made in Rome

Can you imagine not knowing who you were going to marry until the day of the wedding? In Roman times, marriages were usually arranged by parents for political, social, and business reasons. Caesar and Cornelia were probably strangers before their wedding.

The day before the big event, Cornelia probably gave her childhood toys and clothes to the household gods. Early the next morning, she dressed in her wedding clothes and waited for Caesar and his family to arrive. The wedding took place in the Cinna's house. Cornelia was given a small wedding band that she wore on the third finger of her left hand. Afterwards, family members prayed to the household gods and a wedding contract was signed.

Once all of the formalities were taken care of, Cornelia and Caesar hosted a great celebration with a feast and dancing. When it was over, the wedding guests joined in a procession to the couple's new home. It was the law in Rome that their marriage was not final until Cornelia had stayed in Caesar's home for a full year.

CHAPTER THREE
CAESAR ENTERS THE POLITICAL ARENA

While Caesar was busy planning his political career, all was not well in Rome. Despite all of the empire's successes and conquests, the Romans were not happy. As Rome gained more power, certain politicians wanted to make sure they got their own piece of the pie. The senators began to fight among themselves, and two different opinions developed on how Rome should be governed.

The Populares and the Optimates

As a boy, Caesar watched his uncle's rise to power in the Roman Senate. When the members of the Senate began fighting among themselves, Marius became the leader of a political party called the *populares*. The populares claimed to represent the people of Rome. Caesar's father-in-law, Cinna, was also a powerful member of the party.

Caesar never forgot what Gaius had told him: "Rome and the well-being of its citizens should always come first." He knew that winning the favor of the Roman people would help his career. Caesar joined with the populares, and representing the people became central to the way he presented himself to the public throughout his life.

Opposing the populares were the *optimates,* a party made up mainly of upper-class patricians. The optimates thought that they were most qualified to decide what was best for Rome. A man named Lucius Cornelius Sulla (**sul**•uh) became their leader. As time went on, the two political groups could not agree on anything. Both parties were fighting for control of the Senate, and a violent confrontation seemed unavoidable.

The optimates represented the upper class.

The populares represented the common people.

As you may have guessed, it didn't take long for civil war to break out in Rome. Eventually, the leaders of the populares were forced to admit that Sulla and his optimates had won. In the years since the conflict began, Marius had died, Caesar had married Cornelia, and his father-in-law, Cinna, had become the leader of the populares.

The optimates claimed victory by declaring Sulla the dictator of Rome. A dictator is someone who is given complete authority to run the country. The office of dictator was used only during a national emergency.

As his first act as dictator, Sulla published a list of 80 men who were to be executed for their involvement with the populares. The public was horrified, but the next day, a list containing 220 more names was published. On the third day, another 220 names appeared. Each day, Caesar checked the list to see if his name was on it. Amazingly, the young and ambitious politician had been spared. Or so he thought.

Even though Sulla did not execute Caesar, he did summon him and demand that he divorce Cornelia. Her father, Cinna, had been killed by his own soldiers, and Sulla wanted to make sure Caesar realized his ties to Cinna's family would not be tolerated. Sulla thought that divorcing Cornelia would be a symbolic way for Caesar to renounce his allegiance to the populares.

Boldly, Caesar refused to give in to Sulla's demands. No one is sure if it was his love for Cornelia or his lack of respect for Sulla that made him do it. As you can probably guess, his decision did not please Sulla. In fact,

Caesar soon began to fear that his life was in danger. He decided it would be best to go into hiding in order to escape Sulla's wrath. So, after saying good-bye to Cornelia, he took several slaves and went to hide in the hills of central Italy.

Caesar served as a local governor in Asia Minor.

Caesar Joins the Military

To make sure Caesar remained safe from Sulla, his family used their influence to secure a position for him in the Roman army. At the age of 18, Caesar began what would eventually become an outstanding military career. Most wealthy, young Romans typically spent a year or two serving on a general's staff.

However, in this case, there was a more important reason than tradition—Rome was not safe for a young, ambitious populare like Caesar. When Caesar was informed of his family's efforts, he came out of hiding and returned to Rome to gather his things. Then, he said good-bye to his family and friends, made an offering to the household gods, and left home, not knowing if or when he would return.

Caesar's post was in Asia Minor, where he served on the staff of one of the local governors. We don't know much about his time there, but we do know that he distinguished himself while fighting on the front line. Apparently, he saved a fellow soldier from death and was awarded Rome's highest reward for courage, the civic crown. The crown was actually a wreath made out of oak leaves. It was so highly respected that people would stand when Caesar walked by wearing it. For the rest of his life, he wore it at every opportunity.

One day, Caesar received a message. Sulla was dead. Four years after he had left Rome, it was now safe for him to return home to his wife and five-year-old daughter, Julia. The young man who had gone to war returned as a man ready to begin his political career.

Caesar Seeks a Name in Politics

Soon after his return, an opportunity came up for Caesar to make a political name for himself. He knew that he was a talented public speaker. Caesar volunteered to prosecute two of Sulla's supporters who were accused of trying to grow rich at the public's expense. In the Roman courts, any Roman could accuse another of a crime. These accusations were made in long public speeches called *prosecutions*. To ambitious young men like Caesar, they were seen as a way to practice speaking skills and gain favor with the public. For Caesar, making a name for himself as a populare who supported the people of Rome was the perfect way for him to advance his political career.

Caesar apparently impressed everyone with his performance in court except the jurors. He lost his first two cases. It became obvious that Caesar needed more formal training in public speaking. In 75 B.C., he set off for the island of Rhodes where he was to study under the famous rhetorician, Apollonius Molon. Molon had coached Caesar's childhood friend Cicero (**sis**•uh•roh), who was establishing a reputation for himself as an impressive orator.

Pirates

While sailing to Rhodes, Caesar was captured by pirates and held for ransom. When the pirates demanded a ransom of 20 talents, Caesar burst out laughing. (One talent was roughly equivalent to $5,000–$10,000.) He told them they had no idea who they had captured, and he volunteered to pay *50* talents. True to his character, Caesar made himself comfortable while his slaves went off to collect the money. The Roman writer Plutarch describes Caesar's stay with his captors:

He treated them so high-handedly that, whenever he wanted to sleep, he would tell them to stop talking. For 38 days, with the greatest unconcern, he joined in all their games and exercises, just as if he were their leader instead of their prisoner. He also wrote poems and speeches which he read aloud to them, and if they failed to admire his work, he would call them to their faces illiterate savages, and would often laughingly threaten to have them all hanged.

When his companions returned with the ransom, the pirates released Caesar, probably happy to be rid of him. Can you guess what Caesar did next? He rushed off to hire ships and men and went back to fulfill his promise to the captors. The pirates were captured and hanged.

Caesar acted like the leader of the pirates instead of the captor.

After his adventures with the pirates, Caesar continued on his journey to Rhodes. Shortly after his arrival, Caesar got word that another war had broken out in Asia Minor. Without hesitation, he left Rhodes to join the Roman general and his troops. After two more years in Asia, Caesar finally returned to Rome.

Climbing the Political Ladder

Upon his return, Caesar was ready to begin climbing the political ladder, one rung at a time. For the rest of his twenties, Caesar stayed in Rome. He lived with his wife Cornelia, his daughter Julia, and his mother Aurelia in the same neighborhood where he had grown up.

Unlike the powerful nobles in Rome, Caesar lived among the common people. It certainly wasn't his choice—he was broke. Sulla had taken away his inheritance and Cornelia's dowry, or money brought into the marriage. However, it may have worked to Caesar's advantage. Ordinary citizens knew him and felt that he understood the plights of the common Roman.

Unfortunately, popularity only went so far. What Caesar really needed was money. He spent many hours trying to convince moneylenders and senators to invest in his political career. In return, he promised that as he gained power, anyone who backed him financially would receive a healthy return on their investment.

As the Senate fought to keep its power in a Republic where it was supposed to represent the people, many politicians became corrupt. In Rome, every male citizen could take part in elections, but most didn't have time. In order to vote, citizens had to be present at meetings of the Assembly. The Assembly was where the public went to vote and voice their opinions on political issues. Most Romans had to work and were unable to sit at the Assembly, waiting to cast their vote. Consequently, only people who were **idle,** or unemployed, showed up. If someone offered them money to vote a certain way, citizens were often more than happy to oblige. Roman government became a flawed system, where money often had a louder voice than true public opinion.

Republic vs. Democracy

If someone came up to you and asked whether the United States was a republic or a democracy, what would you say? Before you give your final answer, take a look at the definitions for each form of government.

Republic—Supreme power lies in a body of citizens who are entitled to vote for officers and representatives responsible to them.

Democracy—The common people are considered to have the primary source of power to make and change laws.

What do you think? Who makes our laws? Can you or your parents decide to change a law? Of course not. However, you can take your ideas to your state or federal representative or senator. He or she might decide that it is a great idea and turn it into a bill that could someday be passed into a law. That makes the United States government much more like a republic than a democracy.

Our form of government is in some ways very similar to Rome's. The citizens of Rome elected senators to make their laws. In the United States, we do the same thing. However, Rome did not have a constitution to limit the senators' power, and we do. Our constitution limits the government's power and forces lawmakers to rely on the support of the people to keep their vote. The United States has taken the ideas of a democracy and used them to design a type of republic that works more effectively than the one in Rome did.

Therefore, the answer to the question is the United States is a republic that uses some ideas founded in democracy. Some people have even started using the name democratic-republic to describe it.

CHAPTER FOUR
CLIMBING THE POLITICAL LADDER

Despite Caesar's need for money, things were going well for the ambitious politician. He was making a name for himself as a man who cared about Rome and its people. But in his personal life, there was tragedy. Caesar's wife, Cornelia, died suddenly in 69 B.C. After her death, Caesar worked even harder on his political career.

Caesar began to mix with the public even more than he had before. He often did business in the **forum,** the public square and marketplace of Rome. There, he offered compliments and promises of help to the people he met. By playing the role of public servant, he began to amass a large political following.

The Forum

Today, if we want to find out the most current news of the day, we turn on our televisions, radios, or computers. Our common meeting places might be shopping malls or bookstores. If we had lived in ancient Rome, we would have put on our togas and sandals and headed to the forum to find out the latest scoops of the day.

Victory at Last

Finally, his efforts paid off, and Caesar was elected quaestor of Spain. A quaestor (**kwes•tuhr**) assisted the governor with the financial and administrative needs of a **province**. Shortly after Cornelia's funeral, Caesar went to Spain. He was 31 years old.

Being the Spanish quaestor was one of the least desirable positions available. Caesar spent most of his time solving legal disputes in the region. The job bored

Bust of Alexander the Great

The Desire for Power

While there are many sides to Julius Caesar's personality, his desire for power seems to have been a preoccupation that consumed much of his life. There is a story that while in Spain, Caesar saw a statue of Alexander the Great, the Greek general who conquered Egypt and the Persian Empire. He sighed impatiently and wondered how Alexander had managed to conquer so much at such a young age.

From the time he was a little boy, Julius Caesar had idolized Alexander the Great. He studied the history of Alexander's conquests and often compared his own achievements to the Greek general's. Caesar would probably be very pleased to be considered one of history's great military personalities, along with Alexander the Great.

him, but it did allow him to make connections that would be important later in his career. One other positive aspect of the job for Caesar was that quaestors were given lifetime membership in the Senate upon their return to Rome.

After his term was over, Caesar left Spain with a new plan. The road to success, he reasoned, must lie with others who already held power.

Caesar Entertains the Masses

The first thing that Caesar did when he returned to Rome the following year was to get married. It wasn't a marriage of love, but it was definitely convenient. What Caesar needed most was money, and it happened that his new wife, Pompeia, was from a powerful and wealthy family.

Caesar put his wife's money to good use and began campaigning for the office of aedile. An aedile (**ee•**dyl) was a Roman official in charge of maintaining public buildings and overseeing entertainment for the people. It was the perfect position for Caesar because it gave him an opportunity to impress the common people of Rome with spectacular sporting events and win their approval for other political offices.

As you might have expected, Caesar eventually won the election in 65 B.C. While he was an aedile, he did a lot to improve Rome. He decorated public areas and provided the people of Rome with an abundance of entertainment. There were other aediles, but Caesar frequently took credit for the performances. The public was entertained with naval battles in a flooded arena, battles with wild beasts, and stage plays. It gave the common people something to look forward to in their otherwise difficult lives.

However, what the public wanted to see most were gladiator games. In Rome, gladiators fought each other to the death as entertainment for the public. As an aedile, Caesar spent more money on the games than anyone had ever spent before. In fact, he recruited so many gladiators for a series of games that some senators became concerned. They knew that Caesar was trying to influence the public by taking the credit for the spectacular gladiator games. His political opponents pushed a bill through the Senate limiting the number of gladiators that could participate. But, even with a smaller number of gladiators than Caesar had intended, the games were a huge success, and the public was very pleased with Caesar as an aedile.

Gladiators were brave athletes.

Gladiators

Most gladiators were prisoners of war. After their capture by the army, prisoners were passed on to slave dealers, who bought and sold slaves. Once sold, many of these foreign soldiers were sent to schools where they were trained to fight as gladiators.

At the schools, the slaves exercised with weights and were taught to fight with swords. They trained hard and ate special foods, such as porridge, grain, and beans, which were thought to increase their strength. If a gladiator-in-training disobeyed, he was locked in a dark, rat-infested hole and chained to the wall.

During their training, the slaves learned how to fight like a particular type of gladiator. Some were lightly armored and others fought on chariots. There were at least eleven different types of gladiators. In fact, even though they were rare, there were even some women gladiators.

When their training was over, the owner took his gladiators to perform in the games. The night before, a big banquet was held, and the public came to view the men that would fight the next day. On the day of the games, the gladiators marched into the arena. There, they stood in front of the public and said these words: *"Ave Caesar! Morituri te salutamus!"* This was Latin for "Hail Caesar! We, who are about to die, salute you!"

During the games, winning was all that mattered. Owners spent a lot of money to buy, feed, train, and equip the gladiators. Spectators gambled on each fight. If an owner had a winning gladiator, he could become a rich man. However, there wasn't much in it for the gladiators. If a gladiator lost, he died; if he won, he lived to fight another battle.

It was during Caesar's time as an aedile that he became known as the "father of the gladiator games." Even though the public loved them, Caesar showed little interest in the games themselves. In fact, even though he always attended the events in order to take credit for the public's entertainment, he did not watch them. Instead, he spent his time writing speeches and letters.

Now Caesar had the people's support. He was also beginning to gain the support of other powerful men in Rome. Two men in particular became very important to Caesar's future political career. Their names were Marcus Crassus (**kras**•uhs) and Gnaeus Pompey (**pom**•pee).

Political Allies Pave the Road to Power

Marcus Crassus was the wealthiest man in Rome. He made his fortune from silver mines and real estate and used his money to wield power in the Senate. Gnaeus Pompey was a powerful general in the Roman army.

In 73 B.C. a slave named Spartacus escaped from a gladiator school and led a slave revolt throughout much of Italy. Two years later, Crassus, with the help of Pompey, managed to defeat the slave army. By then, the slaves numbered more than 90,000 members. Knowing how much the Romans depended on slaves, you can imagine how pleased they were when Spartacus' army was defeated and captured. Crassus and Pompey became national heroes. The next year, both of them were elected consuls in the Senate. The consuls were the most powerful men in Rome. They were responsible for the administration of laws and the Roman armies.

Caesar knew that at least for the time being, Crassus and Pompey would be important people in Roman politics. As time went on, Pompey gained even more power when he and his armies rid the Mediterranean Sea of pirates without losing a single ship. This incredible achievement gave Pompey too much power in some people's minds. They were concerned that Pompey could someday undermine the authority of the Senate and try to rule Rome by himself.

Caesar, however, admired Pompey's rise to power. Someday, Caesar reasoned, Pompey could be a threat, but for now, he could learn a lot from the experienced general. Even though Caesar had the public convinced, he knew it would be work to further his political ambitions, and powerful **allies** could be very helpful. If Crassus and Pompey supported Caesar, his chances of success would improve greatly.

Crassus and Caesar

Marcus Crassus and Caesar were both members of the populare party. They claimed to represent the people, but by now, you know that it was only a way to get the common people's vote. Knowing what you know about Crassus, can you figure out why Caesar thought it was so important to be allies with him? If your answer was money, you are exactly right. Remember, politics in Rome took money, and Crassus had more of it than anyone else in Rome.

Crassus gladly supported Caesar's political campaigns because they were both members of the populare party.

He also thought his support of Caesar would limit Pompey's popularity and power, which concerned Crassus. Consequently, he was quite happy to help Caesar fund his political career.

Caesar as Pontifex Maximus

After the successful gladiator games, Caesar became a household name. He was ready to move on to bigger and better political challenges. In 63 B.C. his chance finally came. The chief priest, or *pontifex maximus*, of Rome died. The position was usually reserved for a man who had served in the Senate or the military for many years. But Caesar was riding a huge wave of popularity, and he thought he might stand a chance of winning.

With Crassus' financial help, Caesar spent huge amounts of money on the election. To let voters know of his concern for their rights and welfare, he hired workers to paint election posters on the sides of buildings. Those who were not convinced were bribed. It has been said that on the day of the election, Caesar told his mother that she would never see him again if he lost. He had presumably spent so much on bribes that if he had not won, he would have been exiled. It was a huge gamble, but all of the money and bribes paid off. Caesar won by a large majority. The lifelong position of pontifex maximus gave Caesar wealth, prestige, privilege, and an official residence behind high walls in the forum.

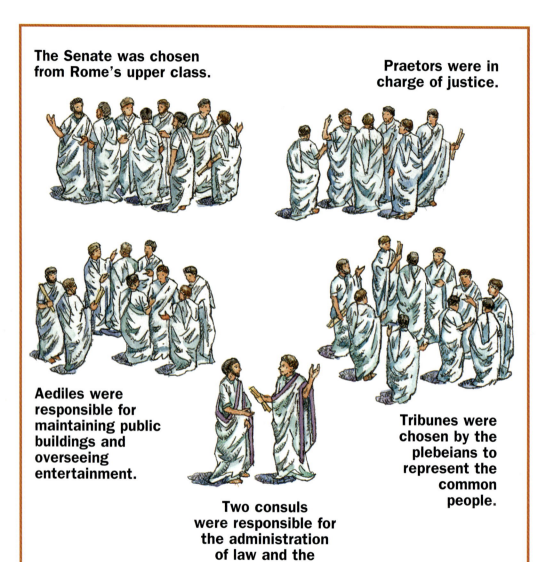

The high walls of Caesar's new home were a symbol of how far removed he had become from the life of the average Roman citizen. As Rome grew over the years, many villagers and laborers began to move into the city. With the steady flow of slaves coming in from successful military campaigns, citizens had a very difficult time finding jobs.

Those who could afford it, lived in apartments, but the streets were spilling over with homeless people. The living conditions were terrible and the people were desperate. They had heard about Caesar and believed he really did have the people's best interests at heart. They hoped that as Caesar got more power, he would implement grain handouts, debt reform, and the redistribution of land in order to make it easier for them to survive. The name *Caesar* represented hope for these people, and he had their support. But as Caesar sat behind the high walls of his new home, he wasn't thinking about grain handouts for the poor. He was thinking about his next political move.

Caesar Leaves Rome for Further Spain

At last, Caesar was out from Crassus' shadow and a leader in his own right. A year after becoming pontifex maximus, he was also elected praetor (**pree**•tuhr), a state judge. It was a prestigious position that brought with it opportunities to make large amounts of money.

As Caesar's power increased, his enemies in the Senate became increasingly concerned. The optimates and populares began to fight about everything. Rome became a scene of mass protests and riots. Politicians were threatened and sometimes battered. The Roman Senate became ineffective because of their bickering, and mob rule began to take over.

During this time, Caesar's wife Pompeia became involved in a scandal. Worried that it might affect his reputation, Caesar divorced her immediately. The marriage had been one of convenience, and Caesar no longer needed Pompeia. However, he refused to admit that she had done anything wrong.

Caesar left Rome to govern Further Spain.

Free from his marriage, Caesar also wished to be free of the bickering going on in Rome. In 61 B.C., Caesar took office as governor of Further Spain, which is now the northwest corner of Spain. He proved to be an excellent governor and a successful military leader. Caesar led several military campaigns that added new territory to Rome.

Caesar got along well with his troops. He slept next to them, ate the same food, and wasn't afraid to fight along with his men. Once again, Caesar proved that he was a man of many talents, and once again, he wanted more.

CHAPTER FIVE
THE TRIUMVIRATE

When Caesar's position as governor was over, he returned to Rome expecting praise and reward from the Senate for his military conquest in Further Spain. But there were many in the Senate who wanted to make things as difficult as possible for him.

Caesar Makes a Decision

Upon his arrival in Rome, Caesar was informed that the Senate would willingly award him a **triumph**. These triumphs were highly prized and allowed a victorious military leader to dress in purple and lead his army, its captives, and any spoils of war through the streets of Rome.

But there was a catch. If he chose to accept the triumph, Caesar could not enter Rome until the day of the parade. In the meantime, the next elections for consul were to take place. Caesar knew he might have a chance to win, but he could not run if he had to remain outside the city walls.

It was obvious that his enemies in the Senate had not forgotten their disagreements while Caesar had been in Further Spain. They knew that choosing between the triumph and the election would be a difficult decision for Caesar. Of course, they hoped he would choose glory over power. So what do you think Caesar did? What would you do if you were in his position?

Even though Caesar desperately wanted to walk triumphantly through Rome with his troops, he chose to return to Rome and run for the election. He was furious with the Senate for forcing him to choose. Caesar knew that the conservatives in the Senate would continue to cause him problems, so he began to look for ways to fight their hold on the government in Rome.

Remember Pompey, the military leader who rid the Mediterranean of pirates? The Senate had slighted him, too. When he returned from battle in Asia Minor, the Senate did not reward him with the land he had been promised for his victories. Both Caesar and Pompey searched for a way to make the Senate pay for their actions.

It didn't take long for both of them to realize that if they joined forces, they could accomplish a great deal more. Crassus had also seen his power slip away in the Senate, and he willingly agreed to help them. On their own, none of the men were strong enough to overshadow the Senate, but by combining their wealth and influence, it was agreed that they could possibly turn the government around to their own ends.

The First Triumvirate

This powerful partnership, made up of Crassus, Pompey, and Caesar, was known as the *First Triumvirate*. In Latin, *triumvirate* means "three men." Its power became obvious rather quickly. With the support of Pompey and Crassus, Caesar was elected consul. The other consul was a man named Marcus Bibulus. Bibulus was a man of little talent, but the conservatives in the Senate hoped he would be able to prevent Caesar from gaining too much power in the position as consul.

Caesar frequently bullied Bibulus into not coming to the Senate. On one occasion, Caesar had dung thrown over Bibulus' head. On another, Caesar used Pompey's army troops to intimidate Bibulus. He had the forum occupied by armed men. When Bibulus came up to speak against one of

Caesar was elected consul.

Caesar's bills, Caesar had him forcibly removed. Afterwards, Bibulus was too terrified of Caesar and Pompey to complete his duties as consul. He stayed at home for the rest of his term.

With Bibulus out of the way, Caesar managed all of the affairs of the state alone. It is important to remember that the consulship was supposed to have two members, in order to keep one man from having all of the power. It became a joke to sign and seal fake documents: "Executed during the Consulship of Julius and Caesar."

Caesar was pleased with the way things turned out. The rest of his term as consul was full of similar types of bullying and intimidation. Caesar was a man who was not above making corrupt deals and breaking laws to get what he wanted. Anyone who objected was dealt with by force.

Meanwhile, the members of the Triumvirate grew wealthier and more **brazen** in their unscrupulous fight for power. Pompey demanded land for his soldiers, and Crassus demanded to be allowed to make money in any way he found appropriate. Caesar gave them everything they wanted.

There were, however, some problems of jealousy among the three men. In order to help bind their agreement, Caesar offered to allow Pompey to marry his daughter, Julia. At about the same time, Caesar married Calpurnia, the daughter of one of Pompey's friends.

As time went on, the Triumvirate began to dominate Roman politics. Between these three men, they had very powerful resources—Pompey's military power and fame, Crassus' huge fortune, and Caesar's growing body of supporters. There was no doubt that the Triumvirate had become a strong force in Roman politics. The optimates in the Senate were very concerned that the Triumvirate was the beginning of the end for the Republic. Many of them blamed Caesar and his popularity with the people. According to Plutarch, this is what the famous senator, Cicero, thought of Caesar:

> *"Cicero, who understood how powerful a character was hidden behind Caesar's agreeable manner, said that in general, he could detect in everything that Caesar planned or undertook in politics a purpose that was aiming at absolute power. 'On the other hand,' he said, 'when I notice how carefully arranged his hair is and when I watch him adjusting the parting with one finger, I cannot imagine that this man could conceive of such a wicked crime as to destroy the Roman Republic.'"*

As Cicero and other conservatives worried, Caesar began to plot his next move. He began to worry about what would happen when his term as consul was over. Caesar had made a lot of enemies in the Senate, and he knew they would be looking for revenge. Right now, Pompey's troops were there to protect him and enforce his will in the Senate. But what would happen if Pompey were as ambitious as he was? It didn't take long for Caesar to realize that in order to remain in power when his term was over, he would need a loyal army to support him.

Caesar As Proconsul

Caesar was very shrewd, and when he wanted something, he figured out a way to get it. One way for him to acquire military support was to be appointed as proconsul, or governor of an important province. Once there, he could build up an army that would be loyal only to him. One other thing that made the job of proconsul so appealing was that Roman law prohibited the prosecution of governors while they were in office. Caesar reasoned that as long as he kept the position, the Senate could not have him arrested for any laws that he may have broken during his consulship.

With a plan in place, Caesar was happy to go on with his political bullying, often resorting to physical violence. He was very quick-tempered and to disagree with him took great courage. As time went on, Caesar worried less about what the Senate thought and did what he thought was in the best interest of his career. To his great delight, Caesar was given two provinces—**Cisalpine Gaul,** in northern Italy, and **Illyricum,** across the Adriatic Sea. When the governor of **Transalpine Gaul** died unexpectedly, Caesar was assigned to that region, too, which includes modern-day Belgium and France. Each province came with its own army, and Caesar was given full charge of them.

When his year as consul was up, Caesar left Rome. Even though his new position as governor prevented him from being prosecuted, things were getting hostile in Rome. Some of the senators wanted to prosecute Caesar

Caesar governed the provinces Cisalpine Gaul, Illyricum, and Transalpine Gaul.

for replacing the gold bars in the treasury with gold-plated bronze bars. In the end, the charges were unjustified, but Caesar knew that there were people in Rome who would not rest until he was destroyed.

Although Caesar was concerned, he wanted to let the Senate know that he wasn't afraid. The day he left Rome, he put on his armor, saddled up his horse, and prayed to the household gods. Then he marched outside the city walls. Once there, he did a peculiar thing—he stopped! As soon as he left the city, the Senate could no longer prosecute him.

Caesar camped within view of the city for several months. He wasn't really sure which province he should travel to, but he knew that he wasn't safe in Rome.

By staying just outside the city walls, he could stay up on what was going on in the Senate and flaunt his immunity from prosecution for just a little bit longer. But in the spring of 58 B.C., news arrived that would give Caesar the opportunity he was seeking.

CHAPTER SIX
THE GALLIC WARS

A depiction of Caesar wearing his civic crown

What Caesar had been waiting for was war! If he were to one day be the sole ruler of Rome, he would need to be as wealthy as Crassus and have a powerful army behind him like Pompey. Caesar hoped that **Gaul** would give him both.

The Helvetii

While Caesar camped on the outskirts of Rome, word came that a Celtic tribe, called the *Helvetii,* were leaving their homes in what is now Switzerland and crossing into Transalpine Gaul to reach the Atlantic Ocean.

At last, Caesar had a war to fight. He planned to stop the Helvetii in Transalpine and show them by force that Transalpine belonged to Rome. So, Caesar gathered up his 60 100-men units, **centuries,** and led his troops into Gaul.

The troops were an impressive sight. Each century marched in line behind their officers, wearing golden helmets with plumes. They carried their battle gear of heavy leather shields, eight-foot javelins, and short-bladed swords. The Roman armies were more organized and disciplined than any other armies in the world.

It must have been terrifying for the Helvetii when they met up with Caesar's army. The Helvetii were a band of 400,000 men, women, and children. They outnumbered the Romans, but they knew that it would be difficult to beat such a well-trained, well-equipped army. The leaders of the Helvetii tribe tried to explain to Caesar that they were not there to fight with the Romans. They only wanted to move their people west, away from marauding Germanic tribes that had been disrupting their lives.

Caesar was not about to let compassion for the Helvetii get in the way of his war. He stalled for a few days in order to bring in more troops. In the end, he refused to allow them passage. Both sides began to prepare for war.

Gathering themselves into a close-grouped formation, the Helvetii charged the Roman lines. They were met by the Romans' eight-foot javelins that easily took out the first line of troops. It was a bloody battle, but the Helvetii were no match for the talented Roman soldiers. Even women and children were not spared by Caesar's army. The few Helvetii that survived were forced back to Switzerland.

Facts About the Roman Army

In Ancient Rome, war was the norm rather than the exception, so huge numbers of men were needed to fight these battles.

- Each Roman legion carried a symbol of Rome's authority. One symbol, the letters SPQR, stand for the Latin words *Senatus Populus que Romanus*—"The Senate and People of Rome."

- Six years was the maximum length of service in the Roman army.

- The draft age was between 17 and 46. Only men who were citizens of Rome could be called to serve (so this excluded slaves and freedmen).

- The cost of the army's weapons was subtracted from the soldiers' pay, but food and a share of the spoils was provided.

- Roman soldier weaponry consisted of pila, or javelins, and a short thrusting gladius, or sword.

- Turtle formation was a popular fighting position that was used by soldiers when penetrating and attacking forts or defending themselves. Roman soldiers grouped together and put shields on their heads and on their sides to protect themselves. When they did this, they could attack forts, and when the enemy threw boulders on them, the boulders bounced off the shields.

To Caesar, the heavy death toll was a small price to pay for victory. By defeating the Helvetii, the Roman army had sent a warning to the other tribes in Gaul. As the news of the Helvetii massacre spread through Gaul, the leaders of several other tribes met with Caesar to assure him that they wanted peace.

The Germans Challenge Caesar in Gaul

One leader was not intimidated by Caesar. The leader of the Germans was a man named Ariovistus. He claimed to be the strongest man in Gaul and was not about to let Caesar take his place. Ariovistus sent word to Caesar that his army would be happy to smash the Romans at Caesar's earliest convenience. As you can probably guess, Caesar was furious with Ariovistus' arrogance. He was determined to put the German leader in his place.

Caesar's troops were not anxious to fight against Ariovistus' army. They had heard stories about how fiercely the Germans fought. But Caesar had proven himself a strong leader, willing to endure the same hardships that the rest of the troops faced. He was not afraid to sleep on the ground or lead his troops into battle.

His army trusted him, and so when Caesar came to address the troops, they listened. He gave a powerful speech to build up **morale**. In it, Caesar told his soldiers they were fighting for Rome and for themselves. He promised that when they returned to Rome victorious, they would be rewarded for their bravery. He described his military plan to defeat the Germans. To show them that he was not afraid, Caesar sent his horse away so that he could stand in the front lines with his troops.

With his army behind him, Caesar prepared to face Ariovistus and the Germans. When the two armies approached one another, Ariovistus and Caesar agreed to meet. The German leader boasted about his powerful army and tried to convince Caesar that the Romans didn't stand a chance of defeating them. Caesar, draped in a blood-red cloak, sat and listened quietly. He was determined to claim Gaul for Rome and was not afraid of a fight to do it.

When an agreement could not be reached, the two armies faced off. Once again, the Romans were outnumbered, and once again, they emerged victorious. By the end of the day, most of the German army had been destroyed. Ariovistus barely escaped and died a short time later.

Gaul and Caesar's Political Image

Caesar himself recorded much of what we know about the Roman conquests in Gaul. Caesar knew he would have to reenter politics, and in order to advertise his greatness, he wanted his version of the conquest in Gaul to be distributed in Rome. In his book called *The Gallic Wars*, he refers to himself as Caesar, so that it appears as though an objective observer documented the events. As you can see by the following paragraph, it was a very effective piece of **propaganda** to send back to Rome.

Caesar had to do everything at once—hoist the flag which was the call to arms, recall the men from their work on the camp, fetch back those who had gone far afield, form the battle line, address the men and sound the trumpet for going into action.

Caesar Claims Gaul for Rome

It didn't take long for Caesar to subdue a large part of Gaul. No other tribes were interested in battling the powerful Roman army. When the news reached Rome, the Senate was delighted. The warrior tribes in Gaul were constantly threatening Italy, and the Romans viewed them as quite a nuisance.

Soon, stories of the battles and Caesar's bravery began to filter through Rome. Caesar sent some of the spoils of his victories on to Rome to fuel his popularity. Among these were gold carvings, silver swords, valuable gems, and slaves. Caesar's conquests also brought opportunities for new jobs in Gaul, new land, and a chance for wealth.

The people were so delighted that the Senate declared a public thanksgiving to celebrate the triumphant achievements of Caesar, conqueror of Gaul. It was to last an unprecedented 15 days, 5 days longer than the one ordered for Pompey after his military conquest in the East.

A Shaky Triumvirate

It was exactly what Caesar had wanted. For those 15 days, he was the hero of Rome. Caesar now had a military reputation, a loyal army, and a Senate willing to honor him. But as Caesar's military career flourished, his political standing began to suffer.

While Caesar was in Gaul, Crassus and Pompey struggled for political power. Pompey was convinced that Crassus was trying to assassinate him, and Crassus was jealous of Pompey's popularity with the people of Rome. The conservative members of the Senate saw the Triumvirate falling apart in Caesar's absence and did everything they could to promote it.

Even though he was still in Gaul, Caesar realized that Pompey and Crassus would be jealous of his conquests. He asked both of them to come to Cisalpine so they could settle their differences. Crassus and Pompey recognized the importance of the Triumvirate and agreed to meet.

They came together in Luca, a village on the border of Italy and Gaul. After a few days of bargaining, the three reached an agreement. Crassus and Pompey would make sure that they were elected as consuls. Once in office, they would pass a law extending Caesar's command in Gaul for an extra five years and grant military commands for Crassus in Syria and Pompey in Spain. Everyone left Luca satisfied, and the Triumvirate was renewed. Secure that the Triumvirate was safe for the time being, Caesar set his sights on other conquests. With Gaul in its place, he looked north to Britain.

The Edge of the World

To the Romans, Britain was a mysterious land located somewhere near the edge of the world. Caesar's only knowledge of the island had been from tales told by sailors who traded goods with its inhabitants, the **Britons**. Their stories of gold, pearls, and silver made the unknown island irresistible to Caesar.

Worried about the arrival of winter, Caesar and his troops left Gaul quickly. Despite their 80-ship fleet, they did not have room for all of the soldiers, and many of them were left behind. Caesar was not concerned about having a small army and felt confident that Britain would be taken with relative ease.

Caesar leading his troops to the coast of Britain

When Caesar and his **legions** arrived in Britain, they were greeted by tribal warriors gathered along the white cliffs of the shore. Caesar decided not to land and ordered his men to sail down the British coast to look for a place to land. When they reached a harbor that seemed to offer less resistance, Caesar's troops waded ashore in full battle gear. Once on land, the Romans had few problems driving the Britons into the coastal forests.

During the next few days, the Romans began to set up camp along the coast. But the Britons did not intend to give in to Caesar and his army. Driving two-wheeled war chariots, they launched a plan of hit-and-run attacks against the Romans. The Britons would materialize suddenly from the forest in their chariots, hurl their spears at the invaders, and then quickly disappear.

The Romans had left much of the army back in Gaul, and they could not defend themselves against the Britons' continuous attacks. Meanwhile, storms with fierce winds and high tides were adding to the Romans' problems and damaging their ships. Some of Caesar's men became convinced that the storms were bad omens dooming the Roman campaign in Britain. Caesar was furious, but after only 18 days on the island, he knew that he had no choice but to return with his army to Gaul.

The next spring, Caesar returned to Britain with more troops and better equipment. This time, he forced the British tribal leaders to surrender. However, it was not the victory that Caesar had hoped for. The British were not easy to control, Caesar did not have enough troops for a permanent military occupation of the island, and there were not enough supplies to last through the coming winter. After only three months, Caesar decided to leave with his troops and return to Gaul. It would be another 100 years before any part of Britain would be under the Roman Empire's control.

In Caesar's mind, however, the battle had not been lost. Even though the conquest of Britain had only been temporary, it was still a conquest! Caesar sent home detailed and exaggerated tales of brilliant campaigns on the mysterious island. To Caesar, military prestige was far more important than actual conquest. As far as Rome was concerned, the mighty Caesar went to the edge of the world and conquered it.

Gaul Rebels

When Caesar got back to Gaul, there was more bad news. Several revolts were in progress, and many Roman soldiers had been killed. Caesar quickly put an end to them with the help of his military commanders, but he knew that he had to do something to keep Gaul under his control. With promises of money, Caesar managed to publicly win some of the **Gallic** tribes back. But in private, they wondered whether it would be possible to drive Caesar and his troops out of Gaul.

Part of Caesar's success in Gaul the first time was due to the fact that the tribes in Gaul were not unified. Separately, they did not stand much chance of defeating the Roman army. But together, they would be a very powerful force. A strong young leader, whose name was Vercingetorix, convinced the tribes of their potential, and they united to form an army to battle Caesar.

Caesar was determined to crush the rebellious army. He and his forces quickly attacked Vercingetorix and his 80,000 warriors. The newly formed Gallic army proved to be no match for the well-trained Romans. Vercingetorix was forced to surrender and lay his weapon at Caesar's feet. He was then taken back to

Rome in chains and paraded around the streets as proof of Caesar's success in Gaul.

There were a few other battles to fight, but after a decade of fighting, Julius Caesar was the master of Gaul. It was a great triumph for the ambitious Caesar. In the name of Rome, he alone had successfully claimed an area that stretched over 20,000 square miles and joined the Mediterranean civilization with northern Europe.

Vercingetorix was forced to lay his weapon at Caesar's feet.

All for the Sake of Rome

The war to conquer Gaul is one that Caesar decided upon for personal gain.

The Roman Empire needed to grow in order to increase its power, and the rewards for military conquest were huge. Hundreds of thousands of people died in the Gallic Wars, but to Caesar, it was a small price to pay for power.

At the age of 50, Caesar was a completely different man from the 30-year-old who had sighed in front of Alexander's statue. He had felt the thrill of victory, and he had tasted the sweetness of absolute authority. It was something he had dreamed about since he was a little boy, and now that he had it, he was very reluctant to give it up.

A statue of Julius Caesar

Who Was Julius Caesar?

By now, you probably have a mental image of what Julius Caesar looked like. How do you picture him? We know from Roman writers that he was a tall man with a fair complexion. His face was described as full with piercing black eyes.

Caesar was very concerned about his appearance. He was always clean-shaven and used tweezers to pull out any unwanted hairs. He was going bald, and this distressed him greatly. To Caesar, his baldness was a disfigurement. He used to comb the thin strands of his hair forward. Nothing pleased him more than an opportunity to wear his civic crown, which he thought covered up his hair loss.

Caesar had a remarkable ability to make himself well liked. Ordinary citizens had great respect for him because of his easy manner and the friendly way that he talked with people. Caesar was well aware of his gift for getting along with people and used it to his advantage to further his political career.

CHAPTER SEVEN

The Civil War

Bust of Julius Caesar

After his exploits in Gaul, Caesar had fame, wealth, and military power. Still some people feared that Caesar, not satisfied with Gaul, would try to seize control of the government in Rome. The optimates in the Senate had not forgotten about Caesar's alleged abuses of power during his term as consul. They vowed to prosecute him upon his return. The prospect of Caesar becoming consul again was unbearable for them, and they were willing to do anything necessary to keep it from happening.

The Triumvirate Crumbles

During his absence from Rome, Caesar had relied heavily on Crassus and Pompey to protect his political interests. But with Caesar away, the optimates tried hard to convince Pompey that he would be more powerful if Caesar were out of the picture. Many senators saw Caesar as a great threat to the Roman Republic. They hoped that even if Pompey came into power, he would still be the lesser of two evils.

While Pompey was trying to gain enough support from Caesar's enemies in Rome, Crassus was fighting a battle against the Parthians in what is now Iran and Iraq. He had hoped that a military campaign against Parthia would help him stay as powerful as Caesar and Pompey. But in a bitter battle, Crassus was killed along with most of his men. The defeat was the worst one that Rome had suffered in 150 years. It was said that the Parthian king ordered Crassus' head to be brought to him on a silver platter. He then had molten gold poured into Crassus' mouth, saying, "You have been greedy all of your life. Eat it now."

Crassus had held the triumvirate together, somehow managing to mediate between the huge egos of Pompey and Caesar. The death of Crassus was all the optimates needed. They did everything they could to help Pompey win over the Roman people. They also ordered Caesar back to Rome to be prosecuted for breaking the law during his consulship.

Back in Gaul, Caesar considered his options. He did everything he could to mend his relationship with

Pompey, but he was not successful. Caesar's daughter, Julia, whom he had given to Pompey to seal the Triumvirate, had died. Without Crassus, there was nothing left to hold the two powerful men together. Both Caesar and Pompey had tasted power, and both of them wanted to be the sole ruler of Rome.

A Struggle for Power

Caesar couldn't have been more frustrated. How could the Senate expect Caesar, the mighty conqueror of Gaul, to stand trial for something that had happened over ten years ago? To a man familiar with power and success, the very idea was ridiculous. In Caesar's mind, he had no choice but to refuse the Senate's request, saying, "I would sooner be the first man in a barbarian village than the second in Rome."

Marc Antony, Caesar's representative to Rome, delivered the news to the Senate. After listening to the letter, they demanded that Caesar give up his troops and return to Rome or be declared an outlaw. A week later, they declared a national emergency and made Pompey dictator.

To Caesar's way of thinking, the Senate had left him no other choice. In order to protect his honor and to save himself from prosecution and exile, he had to declare war on his beloved Rome. Caesar prepared his troops for a military invasion. Just three days after the Senate made Pompey dictator of Rome, Caesar led a single legion of troops across a small stream called the *Rubicon*, on the border of Gaul and Italy. As Caesar marched his troops across the border of Italy, he uttered the famous phrase, "The die is cast." It meant that they could no longer turn back, and the conflict known as the Roman Civil War had begun.

For the Sake of Honor

When Cicero, the powerful Roman senator, found out about Caesar's intent, he had this to say:

> *This insane, miserable fellow has never had the least inkling of the good! Yet, he claims that he is doing everything for the sake of his honor! But where does honor reside, if not in honorable conduct? And can it be honorable to hold on to an army without the approval of the Senate? How can it be permissible to begin a civil war for the sake of one's own honor?*

As Caesar and his army made their way south to Rome, his experienced soldiers easily occupied the cities and towns along the way. Most Romans had heard about Caesar's cruel treatment of Gaul, and they feared the worst. However, Caesar was much more shrewd than that. He ordered that anyone captured should be released and asked not to fight against Caesar again. When people began to realize that Caesar only wanted their support, they found it safer to welcome him than fight him. Their open city gates paved the way for Caesar's entrance into Rome.

The optimates in the Senate were shocked. They had completely underestimated Caesar's influence with the people. In fact, more and more Romans were beginning to think that Caesar had a legitimate claim to power. To secure their safety, the senators fled to Greece with Pompey.

Caesar marched his troops across the border of Italy.

The Beginning of a New Rome

Caesar was put in an interesting position. Here he was in Rome, and all of his opposition in the Senate had fled from Rome with Pompey. Despite the great wealth he had obtained in Gaul, Caesar knew it would take a lot of money to build the ships and fund the army that he would need to fight Pompey in Greece. Because no one

71

could really offer much resistance, Caesar declared that Rome was his to run any way he saw fit. Then, he marched to the national treasury and took the state's money for his own purposes.

The people of Rome were not pleased by Caesar's actions, and he began to be concerned about their continued support. In order to win back the public, Caesar had the flow of grain to Rome secured so that the people would not go hungry during the war. Then he set his eyes on defeating Pompey.

Caesar's first strategy was to go to Spain where Pompey had left some of his legions. It was a short two-month campaign. First Caesar cut off the army's food supply, and then he sat back and waited for them to surrender. His enemies in Greece were stunned once again. Caesar had taken control of Spain without fighting a single battle!

Wasting no time, Caesar headed back to Rome. He was confident that without any opposition from the conservatives, it wouldn't be hard to push through a resolution declaring himself dictator. Claiming it necessary to save Rome from Pompey, Caesar easily got the support he needed.

His first order of business was to address Rome's economy. With the looming civil war, the rich people in Rome began to hoard money. It didn't take long before the supply ran short, and goods became worthless because there was no money to purchase them. To save the failing economy, Caesar forbade the hoarding of money and declared that prices were to return to normal. Within 11 days, public confidence was restored and the economy began to improve.

A Battle for Rome in Greece

Caesar's next act was directed toward Pompey. In the middle of winter, Caesar gathered up his ships and troops and sailed to Greece. Traditionally, Romans refrained from sailing with troops in the winter because the weather could be unpredictable. But the element of surprise made Caesar willing to take the risk. While Pompey was relaxing and finalizing his strategies, Caesar and his army landed in Greece.

Upon hearing of Caesar's landing in Greece, Pompey sent several men to Caesar's camp. They claimed to be deserters from Pompey's army and gave Caesar "valuable" information about Pompey's plans. Acting upon this information, Caesar and his soldiers walked right into a trap. His forces were ambushed, and Caesar was lucky to survive.

After several more months of maneuvering, the two armies met on the edge of a plain near the small town of Pharsalus in east-central Greece. Caesar's army was outnumbered two to one. Pompey and his troops believed victory was certain. They even took time out to argue over who would get Caesar's property. But once the battle began, Caesar took control. By anticipating Pompey's actions and using his reserves at the last minute, Caesar and his troops crushed the overconfident army. Those who weren't killed in the battle were captured.

A Struggle for Power in Egypt

Pompey was left with no choice but to flee for his life. With a few of his advisors, he sailed to Egypt, hoping to find refuge with its young king, Ptolemy XIII.

The Ptolemys, descendents of a general who served under Alexander the Great, had ruled Egypt for generations. Three years before Pompey arrived in Egypt, King Ptolemy XII had died, leaving the throne to his son Ptolemy XIII, age 10, and his daughter Cleopatra VII, age 18. The two children became co-rulers, but because of their young ages, advisors often made decisions for them. Anxious to gain greater influence, the advisors for each sibling schemed to convince their leader to get rid of the other. Ptolemy won and Cleopatra went into exile.

Pompey had supported the king in a battle with his sister, Cleopatra. Unfortunately for Pompey, Ptolemy XIII was not in a position to help him. The king's struggle for power was not over, and he feared his hold on the throne would not withstand Caesar and

A statue of Ptolemy XIII

his armies. If he turned Pompey away, he was afraid that Pompey would ally himself with Cleopatra. Ptolemy's council convinced him that their only choice was to put Pompey to death. A small boat was sent out to pretend to welcome Pompey to Egypt. When he arrived, he was struck down and assassinated.

The Egyptian council had taken care of Pompey, but now they worried that Caesar was not far behind. When Caesar arrived three days later, he was presented with Pompey's head. Instead of thanking the Egyptians as they had hoped, Caesar knelt down and wept. Even though he was glad to have Pompey out of the way, he was not pleased that a great Roman's death had come at the hands of the Egyptians.

In addition to following Pompey, Caesar had another motive for going to Egypt: money. Even with the death of Pompey, he would still need large sums of money to carry on with the civil war. For this reason, he decided to stay in Egypt until he was able to figure out a way to gain access to Egypt's royal treasury. The power struggle in Egypt would make things much easier for Caesar to get what he wanted.

Ptolemy XIII and his council of advisors were not pleased that Caesar had decided to stay in Egypt. They disliked the Roman and feared that Egypt could be next on Caesar's list of military conquests. Cleopatra, on the other hand, accepted the political reality that Rome was the master of the Mediterranean, and it was very likely that Caesar would soon become the master of Rome.

She recognized that a friendship with Caesar could greatly improve her chances for power in Egypt.

Caesar decided to force his way into the Royal Palace in order to avoid hostile Egyptians protesting Rome's presence in their country. As he was settling into his suite of rooms, he had his first encounter with the beautiful Cleopatra, who had managed to smuggle herself into the palace in a rug.

Cleopatra emerged from exile after Caesar forced his way into the Royal Palace.

Caesar was immediately impressed by her bold trick. As he grew to know her better, he was captivated by Cleopatra's intelligence and charm. It didn't take long for these two power-hungry individuals to realize that they could be very useful to one another. Caesar agreed to help Cleopatra gain back the throne, and she agreed to help finance his war after she was in power. In the process, they became close friends.

Once Caesar agreed to help Cleopatra, she came out of exile and informed her brother and his council of her intentions. When Ptolemy XIII discovered Cleopatra had allied with Caesar, he and his council began plotting against them. Rumors soon circulated around Egypt's capital city of Alexandria that the leader of the Romans was attempting to take over Egypt. A mob formed outside the palace walls, and the Egyptian army stood ready to fight.

In the following weeks, the Egyptian forces attacked the palace. Caesar attempted to protect his troops from the siege by sending small war parties into the city to contain the mobs. When reinforcements arrived, the battle moved to the harbor where the Roman ships had docked. After several weeks of fighting in and around Alexandria, Caesar's army finally managed to defeat the Egyptians. In the process, Ptolemy XIII and his top advisors were killed.

Fearful of what Caesar might have in store for them, the citizens of Alexandria begged him for his forgiveness. When he was confident the Egyptians would not give him any more trouble, Caesar accepted their apology and installed Cleopatra on the throne in a lavish public ceremony. To celebrate their victory, Caesar and Cleopatra took a luxurious spring trip down the Nile. Cleopatra showed him the wonderful sights of Egypt in gratitude for Caesar's help in restoring her power.

Caesar and Cleopatra took a cruise down the Nile.

A Final Blow to the Republic

While Caesar was in Egypt with Cleopatra, his enemies had been gathering fresh armies. A revolt broke out in one of the Roman provinces of Asia Minor, and the Roman army was defeated. Caesar and his armies headed to Asia Minor to restore Roman control and defeat the rebellion's leader, Pharnaces.

The rebellion army was no match for Caesar's experienced troops, and the battle was over quickly. In Caesar's mind, it had hardly been worth his time. In a letter to a friend back in Rome, Caesar was said to have described the battle with the now-famous phrase, "Veni, vidi, vici," which means, "I came, I saw, I conquered."

After more than a decade of fighting, Caesar was growing tired of the grueling civil war. This was a war between the crumbling republican government and the authoritarian forces who thought Rome needed one decisive ruler. Caesar and his supporters envisioned a Rome with a dictator who could make decisions for Rome without having to argue with the Senate. To ensure his vision of government prevailed, Caesar would be forced to continue the war until the republican forces were defeated.

Meanwhile in Africa, Pompey's sons, Gnaeus and Sextus, were organizing armies. Caesar knew that he had to organize his troops and head off to battle. Many of the optimates, who supported the republic, joined forces with Pompey's sons. Caesar quickly ended the resistance and returned to Rome.

In July of 46 B.C., the victorious and now unchallenged Caesar arrived in a Rome overflowing with flowers and massive crowds waiting for his return. Over the next few weeks, Caesar was made dictator of Rome and honored with four splendid triumphs for his campaigns in Gaul, Egypt, Asia Minor, and Africa. He sent for Cleopatra and her young son, Caesarion, to join in the festivities.

During this time, Pompey's two sons went to Spain and assembled a powerful army. Fearing them to be a serious threat, Caesar led his army into Spain. In March of the next year, he defeated the brothers in the Battle of Munda. Caesar was victorious once again.

Caesar's successful campaign in Munda ended the civil war. He had proved himself a brilliant general. In Gaul, he had established himself as a superior military commander. In Egypt, he defeated a king and crowned a queen. There were few places left for Caesar to conquer, and it was time to return to Rome and establish a new form of government. Caesar's message after his victory in Asia Minor easily summed up his military career—"Veni, vidi, vici!"

CHAPTER EIGHT
Caesar's Final Battle:
The Fall
of the
Roman Republic

At last, there was no doubt in anyone's mind Caesar was the master of the Roman Empire. Some Romans were hopeful Caesar would change Rome for the better; others feared his changes. As a military leader, he had demonstrated his genius for resolving conflict on the battlefield. But, bringing back political stability to an empire wracked by civil war would prove to be much more difficult.

Dictator for Life

When Caesar returned to Rome, he celebrated a triumph for his victory. This time, he did not have the support of the Roman people. Tradition dictated that triumphs were for victories over foreign enemies. It was not considered proper to celebrate the deaths of fellow Romans.

Despite the public's disapproval of the triumph, Caesar was declared dictator perpetuus in February of 44 B.C. This meant that Caesar would be dictator of Rome for the rest of his life. While he had been named dictator of Rome twice before, it had only been for short periods in times of crisis. The title of *dictator perpetuus* carried with it great power.

Four Kings in a Deck!

According to legend, each of the four kings in a deck of playing cards represents a different great king from world history.

King David is the King of Spades. King David was the king of Israel until his death in 962 B.C. According to the Bible, David won a battle against a giant named Goliath. Today, any unequal contest, where one side is bigger or more powerful than the other, is called a "David and Goliath" contest.

The King of Clubs represents Alexander the Great, who ruled Greece in the fourth century B.C. At one time, his empire stretched all the way from Greece to India in the East.

Charlemagne is the King of Hearts. Charlemagne's name means "Charles the Great." He ruled the Holy Roman Empire from 800 to 814. This empire included parts of what are now the countries of France and Italy.

Last, but not least, is the King of Diamonds. This card represents the great Roman emperor Julius Caesar.

Using his new powers, Caesar began to reorganize Rome's unstable government. The Senate was enlarged to 900 members from many different backgrounds. However, most of its power was taken away and given to the new dictator. Caesar's reasoning for this was to take control of the Senate away from the patricians. The treasury was also taken under control, and it soon began to coin money bearing the likeness of Caesar.

The lives of the plebeians were greatly improved by Caesar's new government. Jobs were protected from being taken over by slave labor, and a massive building program provided work and security for the citizens of Rome.

When Caesar became frustrated with trying to schedule events with a Roman calendar that did not match the seasons, he simply decided to create a new one. The problem was that the Romans used a lunar calendar of 355 days. Caesar added ten more days to the calendar and renamed the month of his birth "July." It was called the *Julian calendar,* and it became the calendar of the Mediterranean world.

Yet, not all of Caesar's political decisions were as wise as they should have been. Caesar was charming, gracious, and well-mannered, and he saw to it that law and order were being restored to Rome. Yet, Caesar acted as he saw fit. Many of his decisions were designed to guarantee him the two things that he had fought so hard for—power and glory.

It didn't take long for rumors to start spreading through the capital that Caesar planned to make himself the king of Rome. Kings had been abolished during the establishment of the Republic four centuries earlier, and most supporters viewed the idea of a king with outrage and horror. Caesar was quite aware of their feelings and used it to his political advantage.

During a public festival in February of 44 B.C., Caesar had Marc Antony offer him a crown. Caesar then made a huge spectacle of rejecting the offer, saying, "I am not king, I am Caesar." He was hoping to prove that he had no interest in being the king of Rome. However, his enemies were unconvinced. Secretly, they began to plot the end of Caesar's dictatorship.

Caesar refused a crown from Marc Antony.

The Plot

With their beloved Roman Republic falling apart at the hands of Caesar, a number of prominent Romans and senators became convinced the only way to save Rome was to have Caesar killed. His enemies had learned they could not defeat him in war, but they believed an assassination would be more successful.

The final decision was made when Caesar announced he was planning to leave for Parthia. A rebellion was going on in the Roman province of Syria. Caesar thought he could give aid to the rebellion and possibly extend Rome's borders to India if he were successful. Once he departed for Parthia, a bodyguard of soldiers would surround Caesar at all times. His enemies knew they were running out of time.

There were about sixty **conspirators** involved in the assassination plot against Caesar. Some of these men had been his long-time friends. The reasons for turning against him still remain unclear. It could have been jealousy, ambition, or revenge, but many theorize their love for the Roman Republic far outweighed their friendship with Caesar. If the Republic was to be saved, Caesar must die.

Two senators, Gaius Cassius and Marcus Brutus, headed the great conspiracy to assassinate Caesar. Cassius was very vocal about his dislike for the dictator and resented anyone who was more powerful than he was. He befriended Brutus, and despite Brutus' long-time friendship with Caesar, Cassius was able to convince him Caesar was planning to have himself declared king.

Cassius also claimed that Caesar planned on passing the dictatorship to his nephew Octavian upon his death. The idea of a hereditary dictatorship was extremely distasteful to the Romans who still supported the Republic.

Cassius' arguments convinced Brutus and the other conspirators to participate in a plot. The date of the assassination was set for March 15th, known as the *Ides of March,* three days before Caesar was supposed to leave for Parthia.

Caesar had been back in Rome long enough that he had dismissed the bodyguards who protected him during the Spanish campaign with Pompey's sons. He had been known to say it was better to die once than to constantly fear death.

When the day arrived, Calpurnia, who had dreamed of Caesar's death, begged him not to leave the house. Caesar ignored her pleas and left home for the last time.

The Senate House was being rebuilt, so the senators were meeting at a theater in Rome built by Caesar's former archrival, Pompey. Along the way, Caesar was handed a letter from a man warning him of the plot against his life, but Caesar never read it.

Marcus Brutus

Marcus Brutus, a long-time friend of Caesar, was one of the leaders who plotted his death. His family history made him an important symbol for the senators. Remember when the Romans removed the kings from their city centuries earlier? Brutus claimed he was a descendent of one of the men who had killed the last king of Rome. The senators felt that Brutus would rush in a new era of liberty and freedom for the people of Rome. After the death of Caesar, Brutus called himself a champion of liberty.

When he reached the Senate, the conspirators were waiting. They crowded around Caesar as if to make requests. In an instant, Caesar's toga was pulled down around his shoulders so that he was unable to fight back, and the conspirators acted on their plot. When it was over, all that was left of Caesar's power was his shredded purple toga in the corner of the floor.

The other senators quickly realized what had happened. Many of them rushed through the doors of the theater and fled to their homes. Seeing the senators so frightened and hearing rumors of Caesar's death, the people of Rome began to panic. Some of them bolted their doors; others left their counters and shops and ran to see if it was really true. The conspirators, still holding their weapons, marched to the forum crying, "Liberty." They were disappointed to find it nearly empty and did everything they could to find supporters along the way.

The plot to assassinate Caesar had not been very well thought-out. The conspirators had not really stopped to think about what would happen after Caesar's death. They blamed Caesar for destroying the Roman Republic and were unable to see it had been the misrule by the Senate that had been the real culprit. According to Cicero, "It was planned with the courage of men but the understanding of boys." The conspirators hoped that by getting rid of Caesar, they could restore Rome to the days of the Republic. But, what they failed to see was Rome had changed, and with or without Caesar, the days of the Republic were quickly coming to an end.

Portrait of Julius Caesar's assassination

At Caesar's funeral, the common people of Rome grieved over his death. When their beloved dictator's **will** was read, the people of Rome learned Caesar had left each citizen a small sum of money and had made his gardens near the Tiber River a public park. The crowds were furious with the conspirators when they found out how generous Caesar had been. The citizens lost all patience with the conspirators and forced them to leave Rome.

It has been said that after Caesar's death, a comet was seen streaking through the skies of Rome for six nights.

The Romans believed it was Caesar looking down upon his empire from the heavens. Shortly after that, a Roman coin was minted with a picture of Caesar and a star behind his head. It was a way for the people of Rome to remember the man who had changed Rome forever.

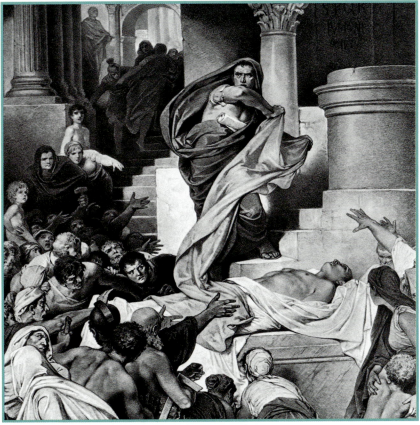

Marc Antony recited Caesar's famous eulogy.

Caesar's Phrases

Three phrases were very important in the life of Julius Caesar. People still use the phrases today—but of course, they are used for slightly different reasons than Caesar used them!

"Beware the Ides of March."

Julius Caesar was warned that he should "Beware the Ides of March." He was told that something terrible would happen to him on that day, the 15th of March. In fact, March 15th did indeed turn out to be the day that he was killed.

Today, when someone says "Beware the Ides of March," it sounds a little bit scary! That's because we know what happened to Julius Caesar on that fateful day. But back in Caesar's time, the phrase "Ides of March" didn't sound frightening at all. The term was actually a very common thing to say. To the ancient Romans, saying "the Ides of March" was just another way to say "the 15th day of March."

"Et tu, Brute?"

History says when Caesar was stabbed and he saw that Brutus was involved, he uttered the words "Et tu, Brute?" In English, this means, "Even you, Brutus?" Caesar, of course, couldn't believe his own friends wanted him dead. The phrase was made famous in Shakespeare's play, *Julius Caesar*.

Today, the phrase "Et tu, Brute?" is sometimes used by people who are surprised or upset that a friend has disappointed them or turned against them. But in such instances, the phrase is usually being used jokingly, not seriously.

"Veni, Vidi, Vici."

Three of the most famous words ever spoken by Julius Caesar are "Veni, vidi, vici." Caesar's successful campaign at Munda ended the civil war. After the very important victory, Caesar sent the message "Veni, vidi, vici" back to the Senate in Rome. In English, the phrase means "I came, I saw, I conquered." People sometimes use this phrase today when they are proud of a particular accomplishment. Like "Et tu, Brute?" the phrase is often used jokingly.

CHAPTER NINE
The Legacy of Julius Caesar

All his life, Julius Caesar had dreamed of power and glory in Rome. As a young boy, he drove his cart around pretending to be a great Roman general. As a great Roman general, he dreamed of ruling an empire. As a dictator of the Roman Empire, he left a legacy that would survive not just for a few decades, but forever.

As you have already learned, Caesar lived his dream. But his road to power required the support of the Roman people, the support of his armies, and the support of his political ambitions. Julius Caesar knew what he wanted, and he knew that he couldn't do it alone.

Caesar and the People

Caesar never forgot his father's advice. He was always very careful to consider the opinions of the Roman people.

Even in death, he knew how to influence them by sharing his wealth with the public. Despite his family background, plebeians, populares, and soldiers often saw him as a supporter of their causes. In almost everything that Julius Caesar did, he considered how the public would react to it and did his best to win its favor. From writing his own versions of military battles, to offering food and money whenever he did something that did not please the Roman people, it could easily be said that Caesar was a master of public relations. By giving Caesar their support, the people gave Caesar power in the Roman government.

Caesar as a General

In his military conquests, Caesar's methods were often brutal and harsh. It is estimated that Caesar and his armies caused a million deaths in Gaul. However, in Caesar's mind, the number of people who died really didn't matter. It was the wealth, the land, and the power that were important to the expansion of Rome.

Most historians agree that Caesar was a brilliant general. His troops were well trained and extremely loyal to their leader. Caesar knew that, as with the people of Rome, it was important to have the support of his troops. By showing them that he was not afraid to lead in battle and to eat and sleep with the rest of his armies, Caesar easily gained their respect. By giving Caesar their loyalty, the army gave Caesar power to expand Rome and defeat his enemies.

Most historians agree that Caesar was a brilliant general.

Caesar and the Republic

The idea behind the Roman Republic was to take away the **autocratic** rule of a king and allow representatives chosen by the people to make decisions about how they should be governed. As you know, it wasn't a perfect system. The upper class often made laws to benefit themselves and ignored the needs of the common people.

Even though it might not have been perfect, it did allow for debate and, at least in theory, the consent of many citizens.

Caesar realized early in his career that the Roman Republic was dying. The wars, the Triumvirate, and the public's confidence in his decision-making allowed Caesar to slowly chip away at the old republican ways. When he finally had enough power to be declared dictator, Caesar used some of his power to help fix things like the economy and the morale of the lower class. Eventually, Caesar gave himself so much power that other ambitious men in Rome felt they had no choice but to end his life.

The Roman Empire at the time of Caesar's death

A New Beginning

After Caesar's death, Rome was in turmoil. The Republic collapsed and another civil war began. But the political blueprint Caesar left behind shaped Rome's future. Eventually, a stronger Rome emerged with a new form of government. For the next 500 years, one man, called an *emperor,* would rule Rome.

The Man and the Legend

Few men have ever achieved the level of power that Caesar had when he ruled over the Roman Empire. But, Julius Caesar was only a man—a man who did great things for his country, and a man who made horrible mistakes in a quest for power. In some ways, Caesar's death gave him more power than he ever could have dreamed of in life.

The name *Caesar* eventually became a symbol of authority all over the world. Many emperors who ruled Rome after Julius Caesar's death insisted on being referred to as Caesar. Governments in other countries began using the name as the title for their own leaders. In German, the name became "Kaiser." In Russian, it became "Czar" or "Tsar." In Arabic, it was "Qaysar." Although power was something difficult to hold on to during his lifetime, Julius Caesar would probably be very pleased to know that all over the world, his name has become synonymous with the one thing that he had worked for all of his life—power.

How Do We Know?

Julius Caesar was born more than 2,000 years ago. There was no television, no radio, and no printing press. Any information that was recorded about his life had to be written by hand. Despite the hard work that went into making a book back then, several Roman writers took the time to record the events of Julius Caesar's life.

Have you ever played a game called *telephone*? One person starts the game by whispering information to another person in the room. As the game goes on, other players relay the message until everyone has heard it. By the end of the game, the message is usually nothing like it was when the first person started. The game is very similar to what happened after Caesar's death. Everyone was talking about Caesar. Rumors became mixed with facts, and there was really no record of what the truth was.

A man named Suetonius was one of Caesar's most famous biographers. He was in charge of the imperial archives under the emperor Hadrian, about 150 years after Caesar's death. Because of his job, Suetonius had access to some of the best information available about Roman rulers. He wrote a book called *The Twelve Caesars,* which served as a biography for Julius Caesar and the 11 emperors who followed him. Suetonius did his best to sort out the rumors from the truth. His accounts of Julius Caesar's life are some of the best we have.

Another biographer of Caesar's was Plutarch. Plutarch came from a wealthy Greek family and spent much of his time writing about the Romans. In his book *Fall of the Roman Republic*, Plutarch writes about six of the men who contributed to the fall of the Republic. You probably already know who they are: Marius, Sulla, Crassus, Pompey, Caesar, and Cicero.

These two writers and Caesar's own account of the Gallic Wars provide us with much of the information we have about the life and times of Julius Caesar. However, some historians question the accuracy of Plutarch's and Suetonius' accounts, and most regard Caesar's writing as propaganda. It isn't always easy to separate fact from rumor, which means that what happened in Rome more than 2,000 years ago will be studied by historians for a very long time to come.

GAIUS JULIUS CAESAR
TIME LINE OF MAJOR EVENTS

100 B.C. (July 13 or July 14) Gaius Julius Caesar is born to Gaius Caesar and Aurelia

87 B.C. Caesar chosen high priest of Jupiter

84 B.C. Caesar marries Cornelia, daughter of Lucius Cornelius Cinna

82 B.C. Civil war ends – Sulla the victor

81 B.C. Sulla declared dictator of Rome

80 B.C. Caesar leaves Rome for military services with the governor of Asia Minor; Caesar wins corona civica (personal heroism)

78 B.C. Caesar returns to Rome

75 B.C. Leaving Rome to study rhetoric with Apollonius Molon in Rhodes, Caesar is captured by pirates; it takes more than 30 days for his ransom to be paid; Caesar returns and executes all pirates

73 B.C.–
71 B.C. Revolt of slaves under Spartacus

70 B.C. Pompey and Crassus elected consuls

69 B.C. Cornelia dies; Caesar serves as quaestor under governor of Spain; Caesar gives funeral speeches for Marius and Cornelia

67 B.C. Caesar marries Pompeia

65 B.C. Caesar serves as aedile; gains reputation for lavish expenditures on games and crowd-pleasing entertainments

63 B.C. Caesar elected pontifex maximus

62 B.C. Caesar divorces Pompeia; elected praetor

61 B.C. Caesar takes office as governor of Further Spain

60 B.C.	Caesar, Pompey, and Crassus form the Triumvirate; Caesar becomes consul
59 B.C.	Caesar's daughter marries Pompey; Caesar marries Calpurnia
58 B.C.	Caesar becomes governor of Cisalpine Gaul, Illyricum defeats Helvetii and Ariovistus in the first battles of the Gallic Wars
58 B.C.– 50 B.C.	Gallic Wars
55 B.C.	First expedition to Britain; second consulship of Pompey and Crassus; Caesar's governorship—proconsulship extended for five more years
54 B.C.	Second expedition to Britain; Caesar's daughter, Julia, who is Pompey's wife, dies in childbirth
53 B.C.	Crassus killed in battle
52 B.C.	Caesar defeats Vercingetorix
51 B.C.	End of Gallic War
50 B.C.	Caesar conquers Gaul
49 B.C.	Caesar crosses the Rubicon on the night of January 10th with one legion–Civil War begins
48 B.C.	Caesar defeats Pompey; Pompey is then murdered in Egypt by ministers of Ptolemy XIII; Caesar supports Cleopatra in her quest for the rule of Egypt
47 B.C.	Caesar defeats Pharnaces
44 B.C.	Caesar declared dictator for life after victory at Munda; image appears on coins
44 B.C.	Caesar assassinated by republicans, led by Brutus and Cassius, on March 15th

Bibliography

Barter, James. *Julius Caesar and Ancient Rome in World History*. Berkeley Heights, New Jersey: Enslow Publishers, Inc., 2001.

Bradford, Ernle. *Julius Caesar: The Pursuit of Power*. New York: William Morrow & Company, 1984.

Bruns, Roger. *Julius Caesar*. New York: Chelsea House Publishers, 1988.

Caesar, Julius. *The Conquest of Gaul*. New York: Penquin Classics, 1982.

Clybourne, Anna. *The World of Shakespeare*. London: Usborne Publishing Ltd., 1996.

David, Peter. *Julius Caesar*. Indianapolis: Macmillan USA, 1968.

Dupuy, Trevor Nevitt. *The Military Life of Julius Caesar, Imperator*. Danbury, Connecticut: Franklin Watts, Inc., 1969.

Gelzer, Matthias. *Caesar: Politician and Statesman*. Cambridge, Massachusetts: Harvard University Press, 1968 (reprinted 1985).

Grant, Michael. *Julius Caesar*. New York: McGraw-Hill Book Company, 1969.

Green, Robert. *Julius Caesar*. Danbury, Connecticut: Franklin Watts, 1996.

Hinds, Kathryn. *The Ancient Romans*. Tarrytown, New York: Marshall Cavendish Corporation, 1997.

Jimenez, Ramon L. *Caesar Against the Celts*. New York: Sarpedon, 1996.

Komroff, Manuel. *Julius Caesar*. New York: Julian Messner, Inc., 1957.

Matthews, Rupert. *Julius Caesar*. Charlottesville, Virginia: Bookwright Press, 1989.

May, Robin. *Life and Times of Julius Caesar and the Romans*. New York: Franklin Watts, Inc., 1985.

Nardo, Don. *Caesar's Conquest of Gaul*. San Diego, California: Lucent Books, 1996.

Nardo, Don. *The Importance of Julius Caesar*. San Diego, California: Lucent Books, 1997.

Ochoa, George. *The Assassination of Julius Caesar*. Englewood Cliffs, New Jersey: Silver Burdett Press, Inc., 1996.

Platt, Richard. *Julius Caesar: Great Dictator of Rome*. New York: Dorling Kindersley, 2001.

Plutarch. *Fall of the Roman Republic*. New York: Penquin Classics, 1972.

Ridd, Stephen. *Julius Caesar in Gaul and Britain*. Austin, Texas: Raintree Steck-Vaughn, 1995.

Robinson, Charles Alexander. *Ancient Rome*. Danbury, Connecticut: Franklin Watts, 1984.

Stanley, Diane. *Cleopatra*. New York: William Morrow & Company, 1994.

Suetonius. *The Twelve Caesars*. New York: Penquin Classics, 1989.

Web Sites

http: www.infoplease.com/ce6/people/A0857104.html

http: www.greenheart.com/billh/julian.html

http: www.vroma.org/~bmcmanus/caesar.html

http://home.echo-on.net/~smithda/juliuscaesar.html

http://www.historyguide.org/ancient/caesar.html

http://myron.sjsu.edu/romeweb/EMPCONT/e022.htm

http://www.athenapub.com/caesarg1.htm

Glossary

allies (**al**•eyez) a group of people united for some special purpose

autocratic (aw•tuh•**krat**•ik) having absolute power or authority

brazen (**bray**•zuhn) having no shame

Britons (**bri**•tuhnz) Celtic people that inhabited Britain

bust (bust) a sculpture of a person's head, shoulders, and upper chest

centuries (**sen**•chuh•reez) groups of 100 Roman soldiers

Cisalpine Gaul (sis•**al**•pyn gawl) an area of Gaul between the Alps and the Apennines

civil war (**siv**•uhl wor) a war between opposing groups of citizens of one nation

conspirators (kuhn•**speer**•uh•tuhrz) people who plan together secretly to do something illegal or wrong

forum (**for**•uhm) the public square or marketplace in ancient Rome

Gallic (**gal**•ik) relating to Gaul

Gaul (gawl) a territory roughly equivalent to modern France and Belgium

idle (**eye**•dl) doing nothing; not busy

Illyricum (i•**leer**•i•kuhm) a region now part of Yugoslavia and Albania

legions (**lee**•juhnz) army battalions, consisting of about 5,000 men

morale (muh•**ral**) the state of the spirits of a person or group

omens (**oh**•muhnz) occurrences believed to be signs of future good or evil

pagan (**pay**•guhn) a person who is not Christian, Muslim, or Jewish; a person who worships many gods

propaganda (prop•uh•**gan**•duh) systematic efforts to spread opinions or beliefs

province (**prov**•ins) a division of the Roman Empire

republic (ri•**pub**•lik) a government run by representatives chosen by a body of citizens

rhetorician (ret•uh•**rish**•uhn) a person who practices the art of public speaking

Transalpine Gaul (trans•**al**•pyn gawl) an area of Gaul northwest of the Alps

triumph (**treye**•uhmf) a public celebration for a victorious commander and his army

will (wil) a legal document stating what one wishes to be done with his or her property after his or her death

INDEX

A.D. 19
aedile 36–38, 42
Alexander the Great 74, 82
Antony, Marc 69, 84, 89
Ariovistus 57–58
Asia Minor 27–28, 94
assassination 1, 75, 85–87
B.C. 19
Bibulus, Marcus 48–49
Britain . . . . iv, 45, 52, 60–62, 94
Brutus, Marcus 85–86, 90
Calpurnia 49, 86
Cassius, Gaius 85–86
Charlemagne 82
Cicero 50, 70, 87, 96
Cinna, Lucius Cornelius 23–24, 26
Cisalpine Gaul . . . . iv, 51–52, 60
class system 4–6, 11, 18
Cleopatra 74–79
consul 4, 39, 42, 46, 48–51, 60, 67
Cornelia 23, 26–28, 31, 34–35
Crassus, Marcus 39–41, 43, 47–50, 54,
                                         59–60, 68–69, 96
David, King 82
education 10–11, 20

104

Egypt	74–80, 94
equites	5, 11
family	9–12
Further Spain	44–47
Gaul	iv, 45, 52, 54–55, 57–65, 67–69, 71, 79–80, 92, 94
gladiator	37–38
Greece	iv, 27, 72–73, 94
Helvetii	iv, 55–57
housing	6–9
Illyricum	iv, 51–52
Italy	45, 71, 82
Julia (Caesar's daughter)	28, 31, 49, 69
Julian calendar	83
Julii (clan)	19
Juvenal	7
legacy	91–95
Marius, Gaius	19, 24, 26, 96
Molon, Apollonius	29
Munda	80, 90
optimates	24–26, 43, 50, 67–68, 71, 79
patrician	4–5, 11, 17–18, 25, 83
pedagogues	10–11
Pharnaces	78
pirates	29–31, 40, 47

plebeians 5, 7, 11, 16, 83
Plutarch 29, 50, 96
Pompeia 36, 44
Pompey 39–41, 48–51, 54, 59–60,
68–69, 71–75, 79–80, 96
pontifex maximus 41, 43
populares 24–26, 28–29, 40, 44
praetor 42–43
proconsul 51
prosecutions 29
Ptolemy XIII 74–75, 77
quaestor 35
religion 12–13
Remus 3
Rhodes 29, 31
Romulus 3
Senate 1, 4–5, 17, 19, 21, 23–25, 31, 36–37
39–41, 42–44, 46–53, 59–60, 69–71,
79, 83, 86–87, 90
Spartacus 39
Sulla, Lucius Cornelius 25–28, 31, 96
Transalpine Gaul 51–52, 55
Triumvirate 48–50, 59–60, 68–69, 94
Venus 19
Vercingetorix 63–64